Ten P
about

ex libris

Candlestick Press

Published by:

Candlestick Press,
Diversity House, 72 Nottingham Road, Arnold, Nottingham NG5 6LF
www.candlestickpress.co.uk

Design and typesetting by Craig Twigg

Printed by Ratcliff & Roper Print Group, Nottinghamshire, UK

Selection and Introduction © Sean O'Brien, 2022

Cover illustration © Sam Cannon, 2022
www.samcannonart.co.uk

Candlestick Press monogram © Barbara Shaw, 2008

© Candlestick Press, 2022

ISBN 978 1 907598 90 6

Acknowledgements

The poems in this pamphlet are reprinted from the following books, all by
permission of the publishers listed unless stated otherwise. Every effort has been
made to trace the copyright holders of the poems published in this book. The
editor and publisher apologise if any material has been included without
permission or without the appropriate acknowledgement, and would be glad to be
told of anyone who has not been consulted.

Thanks are due to all the copyright holders cited below for their kind permission:

Rita Dove, *The Yellow House on the Corner* (Carnegie Mellon Press, 1989).
Alistair Elliot, *The Real Poems* (Shoestring Press, 2008). Linda France, first
published here, by kind permission of the author. Patrick Kavanagh, *Collected
Poems*, edited by Antoinette Quinn (Allen Lane, 2004), by kind permission of the
Trustees of the Estate of the late Katherine B. Kavanagh, through the Jonathan
Williams Literary Agency. Hannah Lowe, *Chan* (Bloodaxe Books, 2016)
www.bloodaxebooks.com. Caitríona O'Reilly, *The Nowhere Birds* (Bloodaxe
Books, 2001) www.bloodaxebooks.com. Louis Simpson, *Voices in the Distance:
Selected Poems* (Bloodaxe Books; BOA Editions, 2010). Tamar Yoseloff,
Barnard's Star (Enitharmon Press, 2004).

All permissions cleared courtesy of Swift Permissions
swiftpermissions@gmail.com

Where poets are no longer living, their dates are given.

Introduction

History is a very large word for a small anthology to employ. It's hard to find anything that isn't in some way connected to history. Kings and queens, empires and discoveries, war, catastrophe, reform, revolution – these tend to claim the headlines, but everyone who ever lived has spent their days in history, and in recent times local, personal experience has also been given some of the attention it deserves.

In choosing poems to include I've tried to balance issues of global prominence – the discovery of the Americas in Louis Simpson's 'To the Western World', or slavery, depicted in Rita Dove's prose poem 'Kentucky, 1833' – with a sense of the human scale of events and memories evoked in Linda France's 'China, Blue and White' and, in a different way, in Hannah Lowe's 'Ship-breaking.' In Alistair Elliot's 'Buxtehude's Daughter', a poem as rich and as complex in mood as a novel, we hear a voice that history itself might have forgotten, speaking from the meeting-place of fame and anonymity.

I've also tried to remember that our history is neither neutral nor immune to influence. For the anonymous medieval author of 'Adam lay ybounden' human time was inseparable from religious belief, while Caitríona O'Reilly reflects on our ineradicable myth-making habits in 'A Brief History of Light' – a theme at which Patrick Kavanagh's 'Epic' also looks, in its slyly humorous way. Tamar Yoseloff's witty elegy 'The Last Woolworths in America' suggests how even what has seemed indisputably modern – mass consumerism – must fade and decay.

And of course human history is only part of the larger history of Earth, while Earth itself might be seen as a time-capsule in which everything is inserted as a sample handed forward to oblivion. Everything belongs and has its place and time and destination, and one thing that never fails is the fascination of seeing how it came about and what became of it.

Sean O'Brien

A History

When frost and fog are gone to heaven
those far hills are far enough and more.

And yet, men say, still further off
the forests march against the Scots.

It is nobody's country.
                              When the rooks
perform their barebones offices

the flinty blackness of their chant
strikes sparks from the bitter air.

Wise to say nothing of fire or God.

While we are labouring, the sun
in all his arctic splendour

passes over, casting our shadows
like graves on the iron fields.

We're patched and nailed, got up
from dreams and hearsay, scraps of songs

and what this sudden solitary rider shouts
as he goes flying southward in the dusk.

Sean O'Brien

A Brief History of Light

And the light shineth in darkness;
and the darkness comprehended it not.

The dazzle of ocean was their first infatuation,
its starry net, and the fish that mirrored it.
They knew enough to know it was not theirs.
Over the hill a dozen furnaces glowed,
the gold gleamed that was smelted in secret,
and the trapped white light shone bitterly
at the heart of the hardest stone on earth.
But they knew enough to know it was not theirs.
Then their hoards of light grew minor,
since none could view the sun straightly,
and jealousy burned their lives to the core.
So they made a god of it, shedding glory,
shedding his light on all their arguments.
Did they know enough to know it was not theirs?
The god in his wisdom preceded them westwards,
and the forests, in whose pillared interiors
black shapes dwelled, were banished for good.
They promised an end to primitive darkness:
soon there was nothing that was not known.
They thought: *Our light is made, not merely reflected –*
even the forked lightning we have braided!
And they banished the god from the light of their minds.
But they mistook the light for their knowledge of the light,
till light, and only light, was everywhere.
And they vanished in this, their last illumination,
knowing barely enough to know it was not theirs.

Caitríona O'Reilly

'Adam lay ybounden'

Adam lay ybounden, bounden in a bond;
Four thousand winter thought he not too long;

And all was for an apple, an apple that he took,
As clerkes finden, written in their book.

Ne had the apple taken been, the apple taken been,
Ne had never Oure Ladie abeen heav'ne Queen.

Blessed be the time that apple taken was:
Therefore we mown singen. *Deo Gratias.*

Anonymous, 15th century

Epic

I have lived in important places, times
When great events were decided: who owned
That half a rood of rock, a no-man's land
Surrounded by our pitchfork-armed claims.
I heard the Duffys shouting 'Damn your soul'
And old McCabe, stripped to the waist, seen
Step the plot defying blue cast-steel –
'Here is the march along these iron stones'.
That was the year of the Munich bother. Which
Was more important? I inclined
To lose my faith in Ballyrush and Gortin
Till Homer's ghost came whispering to my mind.
He said: I made the *Iliad* from such
A local row. Gods make their own importance.

Patrick Kavanagh (1904 – 1967)

China, Blue and White

We rescue muddy notes
sent by our grandmothers

from soil that swallows
soil that rots:

> *your plates and cups*
> *already broken*

glaze veined
with grains of dirt

archivists of our own lives
do we save ourselves

from ourselves
hands turning blue

bones showing through
clay born from earth

gone back to earth
cast away

where is it –
this *away?*

Linda France

Buxtehude's Daughter

Father would say I thought Orlando Lasso
Was an epic on the old age of a hero –
He teased me horribly. But he also tried
To leave me safe and settled when he died,
Offering my hand in marriage to the best
Who came to take his seat – the musical test,
Then me, the princess of this fairy tale.
That's what he thought. To me, I was for sale
Like fading goods in a window, in our house
Sewing, to show I'd make a model spouse.

When Handel came, he found me elderly.
He was eighteen and I was twenty-eight –
The sad arithmetic of too soon, too late...
I wonder if he ever thinks of me
At night, in London. He liked my soup that day.
Strange to know someone famous far away.

Then young Bach came. He was so keen to learn
He overstayed, and I began to burn
Like a ripe candle in my room alone
Along the corridor. Which he must have known.
Father and he became so close. He knew
The parent's hope – but never called me Du.
Three months I was for sale and was not bought.

Though absent in the wood of musical thought
He must have seen my shape, at meals, because
Unwittingly I fired him for his cousin,
The young and merry one who sang.
                                    And then

Father no longer walked, but flew to heaven.
I still kept house, now for his deputy.
They offered him the job and he took me,
That autumn. So I moved into the bed
Where I was born, and gave my maidenhead
In the same place – where I expect to die.

We have a cat and dog. Johann and I
Named them from operas he composed before
We met: Medea, the Euripidean whore,
And Alaric, the Gothic king. Johann
Christian Schieferdecker ist mein Mann,
Natürlich jünger – just four years, this time.
And do you ask if we had children? Nein.

I made the Elders give Johann more pay:
Organists wear their trouser-seats away –
All that sliding along the bench, you know.
When he plays Bach, he sweats a bit. I glow.

Alistair Elliot (1932 – 2018)

To the Western World

A siren sang, and Europe turned away
From the high castle and the shepherd's crook.
Three caravels went sailing to Cathay
On the strange ocean, and the captains shook
Their banners out across the Mexique Bay.

And in our early days we did the same.
Remembering our fathers in their wreck
We crossed the sea from Palos where they came
And saw, enormous to the little deck,
A shore in silence waiting for a name.

The treasures of Cathay were never found.
In this America, this wilderness
Where the axe echoes with a lonely sound,
The generations labor to possess
And grave by grave we civilize the ground.

Louis Simpson (1923 – 2012)

Kentucky, 1833

It is Sunday, day of roughhousing. We are let out in the woods. The young boys wrestle and butt their heads together like sheep – a circle forms; claps and shouts fill the air. The women, brown and glossy, gather round the banjo player, or simply lie in the sun, legs and aprons folded. The weather's an odd monkey – any other day he's on our backs, his cotton eye everywhere; today the light sifts down like the finest cornmeal, coating our hands and arms with a dust. God's dust, old woman Acker says. She's the only one who could read to us from the Bible, before Massa forbade it. On Sundays something hangs in the air, a hallelujah, a skitter of brass, but we can't call it by name and it disappears.

Then Massa and his gentleman friends come to bet on the boys. They guffaw and shout, taking sides, red-faced on the edge of the boxing ring. There is more kicking, butting, and scuffling – the winner gets a dram of whiskey if he can drink it all in one swig without choking.

Jason is bucking and prancing about – Massa said his name reminded him of some sailor, a hero who crossed an ocean, looking for a golden cotton field. Jason thinks he's born to great things – a suit with gold threads, vest and all. Now the winner is sprawled out under a tree and the sun, that weary tambourine, hesitates at the rim of the sky's green light. It's a crazy feeling that carries through the night; as if the sky were an omen we could not understand, the book that, if we could read, would change our lives.

Rita Dove

The Last Woolworths in America

has a lunch counter that serves strawberry shakes
and grilled cheese on white flattened like a dime
with dill pickle and coleslaw on the side.
The cook slaps another burger on the fire, his apron
pristine, his face, reflected in the chrome, always smiling.
The cashiers too are smiling, each behind
her shining register, cracking open a column
of new nickels, and you know there will never be anywhere
in the world like this again, a place where nothing is over
fifty, the neat aisles with their red signs pointing you
to cosmetics, candy, feminine hygiene, everything
you need. They have been hoarding stuff
that disappeared long ago in other stores:
packets of Space Dust that will fizz purple on your tongue,
old-style Bazooka gum, with an Archie comic inside
and offers for pen knives or kerosene lamps
if you send 800 wrappers and a twenty-cent stamp.
Tubs of maraschino cherries (green ones),
Magic Eight Balls that tell your fortune, Play-Doh,
Lincoln Logs (not Lego), they have been hoarding it
for this: the day they close their doors for good.
What if we were to take to the aisles in protest,
occupy those metal folding chairs, the ones
that leave lattice patterns on your thighs,
a pitcher of Kool-Aid by our side, until they come
to drag us away? But the doors will close today,
there is nothing we can do. The traffic will stop
on Broad Street, other shopkeepers will bow their heads,
the slow procession will move forward, and keep moving
until they are dead, until this street is empty,
and through the big plate glass window,
ghosts play Henry Mancini and Laurence Welk,

the ghost cook will stoke the fire with a vat
of grease and serve up a black plate special
for a blue rinse lady, damned to this spot
for eternity, a skeleton in a paisley dress,
rats begging for scraps at her feet.

Tamar Yoseloff

Ship-breaking

These folks were not the victims of migration… these folks mean to survive – Stuart Hall

I watch old films of shipyards on the Clyde:
cranes ripping ships apart, their metal hides
peeled back by men in goggles wielding fire.
The shock of innards: girders, joists and wires,
a rusted funnel toppling in slow motion.
Those open flanks rain down the cabin's foreign
detritus of flags and posters, turquoise charts
of distant oceans, photographs of sweethearts –

They tore the *Ormonde* up in '52
for scrap. I google what I can. If you
were here, you'd ask me why I care so much.
I'd say it's what we do these days, Dad – clutch
at history. I find old prints – three orphans
on a deckchair squinting at the sun; a crewman
with an arm around a girl, both smiling, windswept;
a stark compartment where you might have slept

and I recall that old trunk in our attic –
cracked leather, rusted clasps – *my box of tricks*
you said, you said you'd lost the only key.
Your home, the ship you sailed, those miles of sea
were locked inside. And now my mind replays
a ciné-film: the young man on a gangway –
the trilby tilted, pocket hankie, his smartest gear
and his stride so well-rehearsed – it says *I'm here.*

Hannah Lowe